Get Acquainted With Your

Christian Faith

Kent Millard

INTRODUCTION

Christian Faith–Belief in Jesus as Christ, following the religion based on the life and teachings of Jesus, manifesting the qualities or spirit of Jesus.

(The American Heritage Dictionary)

A young man visited a Christian worship service for the first time on an Easter Sunday morning. He was intrigued with the singing, the prayers, and the preaching and asked many questions about what each part of the worship service meant. Finally, he asked, "What do Christians believe anyway?"

Could you answer the young man's question? Why or why not?

How would you summarize the basic beliefs and practices of the Christian faith in a few sentences?

If you want to play basketball, you need to learn certain fundamentals about dribbling, passing, and shooting before you can get into the game. If you want to be a writer, you must master certain fundamentals about spelling, punctuation, and grammar before you can write a novel. If you want to live a life of faith, you need to grasp certain fundamental beliefs and practices as you grow in your relationship with God.

While the many different Christian denominations emphasize different aspects of the faith, the vast majority of Christians hold certain basic beliefs in common. This book will help you summarize these basic, fundamental beliefs and practices of the Christian faith.

Jesus' Summary

A lawyer once asked Jesus to summarize his faith: "Teacher, which commandment in the law is the greatest?" Jesus replied: " 'You shall love the Lord your God with all your heart, and with all your soul, and with all your mind.'. . . And . . . 'You shall love your neighbor as yourself' " (Matthew 22:36-39).

With his response, Jesus began the tradition of seeking to summarize what we believe in a few brief words.

An Early Christian Summary

Early Christians also sought to summarize the whole faith in a few words, so they began to write creeds. For example, the Apostles' Creed, one of the oldest creeds of the church, abbreviates the faith in four brief sentences— one about God, two about Jesus, and one about the Holy Spirit.

I believe in God the Father Almighty,
   maker of heaven and earth.

And in Jesus Christ his only Son our Lord;
   who was conceived by the Holy Spirit,
      born of the Virgin Mary,
      suffered under Pontius Pilate,
      was crucified, dead, and buried.
   The third day he rose from the dead;
   he ascended into heaven,
      and sitteth at the right hand of God the Father
      Almighty;
   from thence he shall come to judge the quick and
   the dead.

I believe in the Holy Spirit,
   the holy catholic church,
   the communion of saints,
   the forgiveness of sins,
   the resurrection of the body,
   and the life everlasting. Amen.

A Modern Creed

Nearly two thousand years later, when the first conference of The Methodist Church was held in Korea in 1930, Bishop Herbert Welsh composed a creed that was intended to state the Christian faith in contemporary language and in terms comprehensible to non-Christians. Known as "A Statement of Faith of the Korean Methodist Church," the creed has been used by Christians around the world since 1935. This book will use the creed as an

A Statement of Faith of the Korean Methodist Church

We believe in the one God,
  creator and sustainer of all things, Father of all
    nations,
  the source of all goodness and beauty, all truth
    and love.
We believe in Jesus Christ,
  God manifest in the flesh,
  our teacher, example, and Redeemer, the Savior
    of the world.
We believe in the Holy Spirit,
  God present with us for guidance, for comfort,
    and for strength.
We believe in the forgiveness of sins,
  in the life of love and prayer,
  and in grace equal to every need.
We believe in the Word of God
  contained in the Old and New Testaments
  as the sufficient rule both of faith and of practice.
We believe in the church,
  those who are united in the living Lord
  for the purpose of worship and service.
We believe in the reign of God
  as the divine will realized in human society,
  and in the family of God,
  where we are all brothers and sisters.
We believe in the final triumph of righteousness
  and in the life everlasting. Amen.*

* From *The United Methodist Hymnal*. Copyright © 1989 by The United Methodist Publishing House. Used by permission.

What we believe in our hearts, we say with our lips. What we say with our lips, we live in our lives. What we live in our lives transforms the world.

outline to summarize the fundamental beliefs and practices of the faith.

Every affirmation in the Korean Creed begins with the words *We believe*.

We means that we join with a community of other Christians living here on earth and living in eternity who affirm these beliefs and are shaped by them. That faith community carries us through when we are in doubt and uncertainty about who we are and what our life is all about.

Believe means to accept something as true or to hold certain views or opinions about reality. We all have a belief system that is the internal conversation we have about life. What we say we believe about God and about life has a profound impact on whether we generate negative or positive energy in this world and how God can use us in God's world transformation work.

An Invitation

So,

- If you are new to the Christian faith,
- If you have not thought much about what you believe about the faith,
- If you are just curious about why Christians believe and act as they do,
- If you have a lover's quarrel with certain Christian beliefs,

you are invited to examine the fundamentals of Christian belief as we explore the background and implications of the statements of faith in the Korean Creed.

Lord, I Want to Be a Christian

Lord, I want to be a Christian
in my heart, in my heart;
Lord, I want to be a Christian
in my heart.

Refrain:
In my heart, in my heart,
Lord, I want to be a Christian
in my heart.

A Covenant Prayer in the Wesleyan Tradition

I am no longer my own, but thine.
Put me to what thou wilt, rank me with whom thou wilt.
Put me to doing, put me to suffering.
Let me be employed by thee or laid aside for thee,
exalted for thee or brought low for thee.
Let me be full, let me be empty.
Let me have all things, let me have nothing.
I freely and heartily yield all things
to thy pleasure and disposal.
And now, O glorious and blessed God,
Father, Son, and Holy Spirit,
thou art mine, and I am thine. So be it.
And the covenant which I have made on earth,
let it be ratified in heaven. Amen.

CHAPTER 1

GOD CREATES US

We believe in the one God,
creator and sustainer of all things,
Father of all nations,
the source of all goodness and beauty,
all truth and love.

"In the beginning when God created the
heavens and the earth, . . . God made the two
great lights—the greater light to rule the day
and the lesser light to rule the night—and the
stars. . . . God created . . . every living crea-
ture that moves, of every kind, with which the
waters swarm, and every winged bird of every
kind. . . . God made the wild animals of the
earth of every kind, and . . . everything that
creeps upon the ground of every kind. . . .
"God created humankind in his image,
in the image of God he created them;
male and female he created them.
" . . . God saw everything that he had made,
and indeed, it was very good."
(Genesis 1, selected verses)

We Believe in the One God, Creator and Sustainer of All Things.

Christians affirm that "one God" is the creator, maker, and author of all that is.

The Hebrew people of the Old Testament
were surrounded by other peoples who
believed there were many gods in the world:
—a god of the sun
—a god of the moon
—a god of earth
—a god of fertility
—a god of the seasons.
Some people even believed a different god
had created each of the different races and
tribes of people.

But the Hebrew people were certain that
one God is the creator of everything.

And God Said . . .

The Hebrew people used the same word for
God throughout Genesis 1. They mentioned
every aspect of the world they could think of
to emphasize that that one God created the
earth, the seas, the sun, the moon, the stars,
all living things in the sea, all birds and animals, every plant that grows in the earth, and
all humankind. They also emphasized that
that one God called all Creation good.

Michael Williams tells this story of God and
Creation:

"Before the beginning of the beginning

When a scribe asked Jesus about the greatest commandment, Jesus began his response by quoting from Deuteronomy 6:4: "Hear, O Israel: the Lord our God, the Lord is one" (Mark 12:29).

of anything that ever was there was God and there was nothing. The emptiness was emptier than anyone could imagine.

"So God began to tell the story that became the universe, saying, 'Once upon a time there was light.' And there *was* light. Then God named the light day and the darkness night, the first two characters in the story. And at the end of the first day God said, 'This is great.'

"Then God continued the story, 'Once upon a time there was a sky that sat upon the water.' And that took care of the second day.

" 'And once upon a time there was dry land surrounded by oceans, and the land sprouted all kinds of trees and bushes and plants and flowers, all with seeds to reproduce themselves.' And at the end of the third day God said, 'This is great.'

"On the fourth day God continued, 'Once there were two lights, a greater one to look over the day and a lesser one to guard the night. We'll call the greater one the sun and the lesser one the moon.' And so it was. Then God said, 'This is really great!'

"On the fifth day God said, 'Once there were fish and birds and other creatures of the sea and sky, and they were blessed by giving birth to others of their kind and filled the oceans and the heavens.' And when God saw the colors of the fish sparkling in the water and how the birds graced the sky, the Creator sighed, 'This is truly great.'

"The sixth day was a very busy one as God moved toward the completion of the story. 'Then there were wild animals in the forests and jungles and tame ones on the pastures and plains.' But the story was still not complete. Then God had a flash of insight as sometimes happens in stories. 'Let's put a character in this story who is just like us to take care of all the other characters and things in this story. This character could pick up the story and tell it just as I have.'

"So God told of a character who would be the very image of the divine storyteller. The character was like God and came in two styles, male and female. God told the new creatures to care for everything else in creation and gave the green plants of the earth for the human creatures and all the other animals to eat. So God's story that spoke the world into being came to a close. When God looked at all the wonderful parts of this divine story, the Creator's voice boomed across the entire creation like a strong wind. 'Now this is really great.'

"Then on the seventh day God rested from telling the story of creation and blessed the day, setting it aside for rest.

"To this day we humans still gather on the day of rest to tell God's stories and to bless the day, each other, and creation."

From *The Storyteller's Companion to the Bible*, Volume 1, Genesis, edited by Michael E. Williams. Copyright © 1991 by Abingdon Press. Used by permission.

Pause for Reflection

In her book *Learning and Teaching Christian Meditation* (Cowley Publications, 1990; page 61), Avery Brooke suggests that since God creates everything, then everything in creation can be a means by which we can experience some aspect of God. Consequently, we can ponder the beauty of a sunset, the splendor of a rose, the majesty of snowcapped mountain peaks, the marvel of a newborn baby, the face of a dear friend, and discover something about the nature of the God who created all of life.

While Christians may experience God in many different ways and have many different

Francis of Assisi (1182–1226) felt closest to God in the natural world. He believed that all creation is here to praise God:

"All creatures of our God and King,
 lift up your voice and with us sing, . . .
O brother sun with golden beam,
 O sister moon with silver gleam! . . .
Dear mother earth, who day by day
 unfoldest blessings on our way, . . .
The flowers and fruits that in thee grow,
 let them God's glory also show!
O praise ye! O praise ye!
Alleluia! Alleluia! Alleluia!"

From *The United Methodist Hymnal.* Text adaptations © 1989 by The United Methodist Publishing House. Used by permission.

names for God, Christians believe in one God, one ultimate reality, one ground of being, who is the source and creator of everything.

When have you experienced the wonder and majesty of God through creation?

Is there a special place in this world where you feel close to God and God's creation?

What is your responsibility in caring for God's creation?

Creation, Religion, and Science

Some Christians have a great deal of trouble reconciling the story of Creation in Genesis 1 with contemporary scientific views about creation. The Hebrew people were trying to tell us Who created everything. The basic point of the Creation story in Genesis is that the one true God created everything and called it good. Contemporary scientists, on the other hand, are speculating on how creation came about. The purpose of contemporary science is to seek to discover the way the universe came into being without focusing on Who was behind the process.

Religion and science are looking at the universe from two different points of view and trying to answer different questions about it. Unfortunately, some scientists seem to believe that if they can figure out how God did it, then God did not do it. Sadly too, some Christians believe that faith in God will be destroyed if we have a better understanding of some of the processes God used in bringing the universe into being.

When we look at the universe, there seems to be order and purpose in it. Scientists tell us that the earth is ninety-three million miles from the sun. If the earth were closer to the sun, we would all burn to death; and if it were farther away, we would all freeze to death. Can the fact that we are precisely the right distance from the sun for human, animal, and plant life be an accident? Furthermore, the earth is the only planet in this solar system that has an atmosphere; and we just happen to be the kind of beings who need air to breathe. How could such an ordered creation have come about without any divine mind or energy behind it?

"O Lord, our Sovereign,
    how majestic is your name
    in all the earth!
When I look at your heavens,
    the work of your fingers,
the moon and the stars that
    you have established;
what are human beings that
    you are mindful of them,
mortals that you care for
    them?"

(Psalm 8:1, 3-4)

We Believe in the One God . . . the Source of All Goodness and Beauty, All Truth and Love.

After each day of creation in the story in Genesis 1, the Scripture says: "and God saw that it was good." God creates the sun, the moon, the stars, the animals, the plants, and men and women; and they are declared to be good. Six times the phrase "and God saw that it was good" is used. Finally, after everything is created, the Scripture says: "God saw everything that he had made, and indeed, it was very good" (Genesis 1:31). The point of repeating this phrase so many times is to communicate to us that God has created a *good* world.

Many people believe that the world and all matter are fundamentally evil. The visible and material world is basically bad. They also believe that at the core of our being, human beings are fundamentally evil. But the revelation that comes through Genesis 1 is that God

© Jean Kugler/FPG International Corp.

The book *Chicken Soup for the Soul*, by Jack Canfield and Mark Hansen, includes a story about an American couple who went to Bangkok, Thailand on vacation. While they were there, they visited the temple of the Golden Buddha to see a huge statue of the Buddha made of pure gold. A monk at the temple told them this story about the Golden Buddha: Several hundred years ago, Thailand was invaded by Burma. Before the Burmese troops overran the city, the monks covered the Golden Buddha with about six inches of clay to hide this precious treasure from the invaders and then they fled for their lives. Eventually, other monks came and reopened the temple and prayed in front of a huge clay Buddha. They worshiped before the clay Buddha for centuries without knowing that beneath the clay there was a beautiful Golden Buddha. About 1957, Bangkok was building a new highway, and they had to move the temple. When they lifted the statue of Buddha with a large crane, the clay began to crack open. One of the monks looked in a crack and saw something glistening. He began to chip away the clay and discovered to his complete surprise a beautiful priceless Golden Buddha beneath the clay covering. For all those years there was a Golden Buddha beneath the clay, but no one knew it.

(Health Communications, Inc. 1993; pages 69–71)

sees all the material world as basically good and that human beings are especially good because God made them in God's own image. God's spirit—a spark of the divine light—is placed in every human being. God's spark of goodness and beauty, truth and love, appears in every person God creates.

We all sin; we mask that spark of "goodness and beauty, truth and love" and hide it behind the darkness of pride, arrogance, jealousy, fear, hatred, and our other persistent sins. The story of Adam and Eve in Genesis 2–3 tells about the way we distort the image of God within each of us by our lack of honesty, our tendency to blame others for our mistakes, and our fear. The story of Adam and Eve in the garden of Eden is not about something that happened a long time ago. Their story is about what has probably happened recently in our lives if we have been less than totally honest with God, if we have allowed pride to live in our hearts, or if we have blamed someone else for our mistakes. We hide God's image of goodness and beauty beneath the darkness of our sin, but God's goodness and beauty are still there.

If you were to take a beautiful, sparkling, diamond, drop it in the mud, and then pick it up and give it to someone, it might appear to be only a clump of mud in his or her hand. But you would know that underneath all that mud lies a beautiful diamond. As human beings, we often feel covered with mud because of the sins and wounds of our lives. But underneath that mud we are beautiful, sparkling diamonds—the image of God's goodness and beauty.

Christians believe that we are washed clean through acknowledging our wounds, confessing our sins, and accepting God's healing and forgiveness. The beautiful, sparkling diamond within can once again reflect God's image of "goodness and beauty, truth and love."

© TSM/A1 Francekevich, 1995

Pause for Reflection

The tragedy is that some of us live our whole lives only seeing the mud covering and not realizing that there is a sparkling diamond image of God within us. We only see the mud—the woundedness, the shortcomings, the failures. We do not realize that when we acknowledge our pain and confess our sins, God washes us clean. Then God's image of goodness and beauty can shine forth from within us.

Why do you focus on the woundedness, the shortcomings, and the failures within yourself?

"I am not a human being having a spiritual experience, I am a spiritual being having a human experience."

How might you find God's image of goodness and beauty within you?

When have you focused on the shortcomings and failures of others?

How might you find God's image of goodness and beauty within others?

How Great Thou Art

O Lord my God! when I in awesome wonder
    consider all the worlds thy hands have made,
I see the stars, I hear the rolling thunder,
    thy power throughout the universe displayed.

Refrain:
Then sings my soul, my Savior God to thee;
    how great thou art,
    how great thou art!
Then sings my soul, my Savior God to thee;
    how great thou art,
    how great thou art!

Thanksgiving

Lord of lords,
Creator of all things,
God over all gods,
God of sun and rain,
You created the earth with a thought
    and us
with Your breath.

Lord,
we brought in the harvest.
The rain watered the earth,
the sun drew cassava and corn
out of the clay.
Your mercy showered blessing after
    blessing
over our country.
Creeks grew into rivers;
swamps became lakes.
Healthy fat cows graze on the green
    sea
of the savanna.

The rain smoothed out the clay walls.
The mosquitoes drowned in the high
    waters.

Lord,
the yam is fat like meat,
the cassava melts on the tongue,
oranges burst in their peels,
dazzling and bright.

Lord,
nature gives thanks,
Your creatures give thanks.
Your praise rises in us like the Volta.

Lord of lords,
Creator,
Provider,
we thank you in the name of Jesus
    Christ.
Amen.

CHAPTER 2

GOD COMES TO US

We believe in Jesus Christ,
God manifest in the flesh,
our teacher, example, and Redeemer, the
Savior of the world.

"And the Word became flesh and lived among us, and we have seen his glory, the glory as of a father's only son, full of grace and truth. . . . From his fullness we have all received, grace upon grace. The law indeed was given through Moses; grace and truth came through Jesus Christ. No one has ever seen God. It is God the only Son, who is close to the Father's heart, who has made him known."

(John 1:14-18)

We Believe in Jesus Christ, God Manifest in the Flesh.

God, the creator of the universe, cannot be described in human terms. However, we might imagine God as being like a big ball of light and energy. God's light and energy has created everything that exists. Now picture this light and energy flowing into a human being named Jesus of Nazareth. Jesus was completely filled with God's light and energy. When he touched people who were sick with all kinds of diseases, they were healed because God's light and energy flowed through his body into theirs. When Jesus spoke, God's profound wisdom and insight about the meaning and purpose of life was heard in his words. When he looked at people, they felt God's unconditional love and forgiveness coming into their life and making them whole. When people experienced the presence of Jesus, they said to themselves and to one another: "This is what God is like!"

When one of his followers asked Jesus to show them what God was like, Jesus responded: "Have I been with you all this time,

© Tony Stone Images

Imagine God as a playwright—the creator and author of a play. The playwright creates the stage on which the play will be presented and calls it the earth. The playwright also creates all the actors and actresses who perform in the play throughout the centuries and gives them freedom to improvise on the script as they play their parts. For centuries, God coaches the actors and actresses from the wings, giving them guidance, love, and support from the sidelines. However, at one point in history, God, the playwright, writes himself into the script. God creates a person named Jesus and endows him with God's own characteristics of unconditional love, passion, compassion, vision, power, and grace. Jesus comes onto the stage of the drama of life for just thirty-three years and only has a speaking part for the three years of his public ministry. But in his brief performance on life's stage, Jesus demonstrates what the playwright is like and transforms all human history after him.

Philip, and you still do not know me? Whoever has seen me has seen the Father. . . . Do you not believe that I am in the Father and the Father is in me?" (John 14:9-10).

Jesus was a humble carpenter and itinerant teacher, preacher, and healer. Yet, Christians believe that when we look at the life of Jesus, we see what the creator of the universe—God—is like. Because Jesus was fully human, he was fully divine; and this is why we affirm our faith with these words: "We believe in Jesus Christ, God manifest in the flesh."

Pause for Reflection

A songwriter on the album "For Heaven's Sake" wrote these words about Jesus: "He was a flop at thirty-three; his whole career was one of failure and of loss. The thing that's so distressful is he could have been successful but instead of climbing up he climbed a cross. We've fought our way up to the top. We're all considered as successful men of worth. Now what distresses me, is how this flop at thirty-three is called the one successful man to live on earth" ("Some Career," words by Helen Kromer).

Do you agree that Jesus was a flop? Why or why not?

Why did the songwriter believe Jesus was unsuccessful?

Do you consider yourself to be successful? Why or why not?

"He was born in an obscure village, the child of a peasant woman. He worked in a carpenter's shop and was an itinerant preacher. He never wrote a book. He never held an office. He did none of the things one associates with greatness. Nineteen centuries have come and gone and today he is the central figure of the human race. All the armies that ever marched, all the navies that ever sailed, all the kings that ever reigned put together have not affected the life of man on earth as much as that one solitary man."
—"One Solitary Life," anonymous

What are the characteristics of a successful person?

Remembering a Teacher

Most people can think of a teacher who has had a profound impact on their lives. I think of Mrs. Fowler, my high school English and speech teacher. She taught me to appreciate great literature and opened my mind to the insights about life that come through great authors. I gave my first speech in her class and thought I would die. If it had not been for Mrs. Fowler's coaching and encouragement, I would never have given a speech again, much less entered the preaching ministry of the church. She directed the plays and the choir at our school and involved me in both activities. She also played the piano in the small church we attended and demonstrated her deep faith in the congregation and in her life as a public school teacher.

When I reflect on my life, I realize how I have been shaped by a teacher, someone who believed in me more than I believed in myself, someone who saw my potential and coached me to become a passionate, compassionate, visionary, loving leader.

© Telegraph Colour Library/FPG International Corp.

Pause for Reflection

Who have been the influential and life-transforming teachers on your life journey?

How have you made these persons aware of their important role in your life journey?

When have you served as a teacher, encourager for someone else?

We Believe in Jesus Christ, . . . Our Teacher, Example.

Jesus was often called "Rabbi," which means teacher in Hebrew. When two of John's followers began to follow Jesus, they said to him: "Rabbi . . .`, where are you staying?" (John 1:38). When a Pharisee named Nicodemus came to see Jesus, he said: "Rabbi, we know that you are a teacher who has come from God; for no one can do these signs that you do apart from the presence of God" (John 3:2).

When Jesus called uneducated fishermen to follow him, he was acting as a teacher. He saw their potential for growth in faith and committed himself to helping them live up to their potential. He said to them: "Follow me, and I will make you fish for people" (Matthew 4:19).

Jesus' group of followers included farmers, shepherds, former prostitutes, zealots, wealthy women, and tax collectors. These men and women spent only three years listening to his teachings and observing the example of his life. Yet, after Jesus' death and resurrection, they went out and transformed the world. It was said of them, "These Christians are turning the world upside down." (See Acts 17:6.)

Jesus came to his first disciples and he comes to us as a teacher who sees our potential and believes in us more than we believe in ourselves. He serves as our example as we seek to become all that God intended for us to be.

Pause for Reflection

A teacher needs an attentive class in order to successfully teach. Jesus, as our Living Teacher and Example, needs persons who are attentive and available in order to transform us into the kind of persons God created us to become.

How are you attentive to Jesus' teachings?

In what ways is Jesus' example transforming your life?

When we believe Jesus is our teacher and example and begin to follow his teachings and his example, we will be led to discover him as the Lord and Savior of our life. Commit as much as you know about yourself to as much as you know about Christ, and you will soon discover more about yourself as well as more about Christ.

Imagine that you are bicycling down a path in the woods. You come to a fork in the path and have absolutely no idea which fork to take. Then a man appears at that fork in the road and points you in one direction. You take his advice and follow the path he indicates. The path leads you to your destination—to meaning, fulfillment, and joy in life. Later, you discover that the other path, the one you did not take, leads to an immediate, sharp, drop-off cliff. If you had taken that path, you would have lost your life.

Now, you might say that the man who stands at the fork in the road saved your life by pointing you in the right direction. He is your savior because he pointed you in the way that leads to life rather than destruction. Then if you discover that he stands at the fork in the road on a cross, at the cost of his own life, you might say, "He died so that I might live."

Jesus stands at every fork in the road of our lives at the cost of his own life in order to point us in the direction that leads to an abundant life. Jesus said if we try to hoard our lives, we will lose them. If we share our lives, give ourselves for others and for the gospel, we will find life abundant and meaningful. (See Mark 8:34-36.) The path to which Jesus points is a path of surrendering ourselves into the hands of God, following God's desires for our life, and discovering the blessings that are given in return.

Pause for Reflection
Do you trust the man on the cross? Why or why not?

Will you follow his way to abundant life? How?

We Believe in Jesus Christ . . . Our Redeemer, the Savior of the World.

The Supreme Sacrifice

Several years ago, a plane took off from the airport in Washington, DC, in the middle of a blizzard. The plane had just cleared the runway when it crashed into the icy Potomac River. Emergency rescue teams arrived almost immediately to discover a lot of survivors in the middle of the icy river hanging onto debris from the plane. The rescuers knew they had to get the people out of the water immediately or they would die from shock and hypothermia.

A helicopter was brought in to lower a cable with a life ring attached. A man grabbed the life ring. Rather than hanging on himself and being flown to safety, he put another person in the life ring. He repeated that process more than a dozen times, until all the people around him had been flown to safety.

When the helicopter returned to pick the man up, he was gone. He had died of shock and hypothermia and had sunk beneath the cold waters of the Potomac.

When I read the newspaper account, I began to wonder: *How did those people whom he saved feel about this man and what he did for them? Would they say a prayer of thanks to God every day for the rest of their lives for the one who gave his life so they might live? Would they begin to live their lives more intentionally and appreciatively because someone had died for them? Would they give themselves more generously for others because someone had given himself generously for them?*

This story is an analogy of what Jesus Christ has done for us. Jesus gave his life on a cross for all of humanity. As persons who have benefited from his sacrifice, Christians offer prayers of thanksgiving every day to God for what Jesus has done for us. We live our life intentionally and appreciatively because someone gave up his life in order that we might live abundantly. We follow his example and give ourselves generously for others, just as he gave himself for us.

Pause for Reflection

When we say we believe in "Jesus Christ, God manifest in the flesh," we are proclaiming that in Jesus we experience the light and energy of God being present in our world. When we say Jesus is our teacher and example, we are affirming that Jesus is the teacher who recognizes our potential and stretches us to live up to all we can be. And when we say Jesus is our redeemer and savior, we are proclaiming our love for one who gave his life so we might live.

How will you follow Jesus' teaching and example?

How will you thank God for the gift of Jesus' life for us?

O Love, How Deep

O love, how deep, how broad, how
   high,
  it fills the heart with ecstasy,
that God, the Son of God, should take
  our mortal form for mortals' sake!

For us baptized, for us he bore
  his holy fast and hungered sore,
for us temptation sharp he knew;
  for us the tempter overthrew.

For us he prayed; for us he taught;
  for us his daily works he wrought;
by words and signs and actions thus
  still seeking not himself, but us.

For us to evil power betrayed,
  scourged, mocked, in purple robe
   arrayed,
he bore the shameful cross and death,
  for us gave up his dying breath.

For us he rose from death again;
  for us he went on high to reign;
for us he sent his Spirit here,
  to guide, to strengthen, and to cheer.

All glory to our Lord and God
  for love so deep, so high, so broad:
the Trinity whom we adore,
  forever and forevermore.

Fifteenth-century Latin; translated by Benjamin Webb, 1854

Three Things We Pray

Thanks be to thee, O Lord Jesus Christ, for all the benefits which thou hast given us; for all the pains and insults which thou hast borne for us. O most merciful Redeemer, friend, and brother, may we know thee more clearly, love thee more dearly, and follow thee more nearly, for thine own sake. Amen.

Richard of Chichester, England, thirteenth century

CHAPTER 3

GOD
EMPOWERS
US

We believe in the Holy Spirit,
God present with us for guidance,
for comfort, and for strength.

"If you love me, you will keep my commandments. And I will ask the Father, and he will give you another Advocate, to be with you forever. This is the Spirit of truth, whom the world cannot receive, because it neither sees him nor knows him. You know him, because he abides with you, and he will be in you."

(John 14:15-17)

"I have said these things to you while I am still with you. But the Advocate, the Holy Spirit, whom the Father will send in my name, will teach you everything, and remind you of all that I have said to you."

(John 14:25-26)

We Believe in the Holy Spirit, God Present With Us for Guidance.

Shaquille O'Neal, a professional basketball player for the Orlando Magic basketball team, is over seven feet tall and weighs over three hundred pounds. Shaq is known the world over, not only for his great basketball ability but also for his books, movies, and platinum-selling raps. Michael Jordan made worldwide headlines when he decided to return to play professional basketball for the Chicago Bulls, whom he had led to three world championships. These men have awesome ability on the basketball court; but, no matter how great their ability, they both need a coach to bring out the best in them. They both need someone on the sidelines to:

encourage them when they are discouraged,

challenge them to greater goals,

believe in them when they lose faith in themselves,

cheer them on to becoming the best they can be.

They need a coach.

Someone who wants to become a great actor needs a drama coach. Someone who wants to be a great singer needs a voice coach. In order for such persons to become the best they can be, they need a coach.

© TSM/Ed Bock, 1994.

Coached by Jesus

Jesus came among his disciples as a coach. He called the disciples to be a part of his team. He taught them the fundamentals of living a God-centered life in the midst of this world. He challenged them to become all that God intended for them to be. Jesus encouraged his followers when they were down and believed in them more than they believed in themselves.

When the disciples were paralyzed with fear, Jesus filled them with faith. When they were arrogant and self-righteous, he taught them the way of humble service. Jesus was with his team of followers for three years, essentially serving as their coach in the game of life.

But there came a time in Jesus' life when he knew he would not always be with the disciples physically. He told them that he would be going away. He would ask God to send another coach called the Holy Spirit to empower them. This coach would be with them forever. (See John 14:16, 25-26.)

God the Creator=God working to create the universe and everything in it.
God the Son=Jesus, a human being who enfleshed God at a particular time and place.
God the Holy Spirit=God present with us in this moment as a caring coach, comforter, and counselor.
God the Creator+God the Son+God the Holy Spirit=The Trinity.

Pause for Reflection

Have you ever had a coach? Perhaps you were on a football, basketball, volleyball, tennis, track, or swim team; and you had a coach whose role was to bring out the best in you. Or perhaps you were in drama or music and had a coach or director who helped you develop your abilities. While not all coaches are model persons, when they are at their best, they are essential for helping a team achieve its goals and for helping individuals on the team fulfill their potential.

Think about God the Holy Spirit being present with you right now, wherever you are. What kind of coaching do you think the Holy Spirit is trying to give you in order for you to fulfill your God-given potential?

Guided by the Holy Spirit

Recently, I had an experience of guidance that caused me to pause and thank God for the presence and empowerment of the Holy Spirit. I was going to the church I serve after an early morning breakfast meeting and happened to be driving past one of our local hospitals. As I neared the hospital, the thought occurred to me that I should stop to see if any members of our congregation had entered the hospital overnight. But then I thought, *It's not my day to visit the hospital; another pastor on the staff will be stopping by this afternoon and will visit any of our hospitalized members.*

So I kept driving. Then it came again—a strong urging that I should stop at the hospital. Again I resisted. I began to think of the big stack of work piled on my desk at the church office and how I needed to get to work on it, so I kept going.

Then the urging returned like a bolt of lightning; and it was almost as if a voice said to me, "Go to the hospital!" So I turned into the hospital parking lot, went to the front desk, and discovered that one of our church members had, in fact, been admitted the night before.

When I went into Bill's room, I saw that he

Three Ways to Recognize the Holy Spirit's Guidance:

1. Persistence—We may have said no time and time again, but the Spirit just keeps calling us in a variety of ways.

2. Confirmation by others—As we talk to family and friends, we begin to discover they confirm that we have the gifts and talents necessary for the task to which the Spirit is calling us.

3. Risk taking—We are called to take a risk in which we must trust the power and presence of God to get us through successfully.

Terry Vine/© Tony Stone Images

was crying. He said the doctor had just given him some bad news: "The cancer is back and growing rapidly. There are no more treatments we can give you. Now it's just a matter of time." Then Bill looked at me intently and said through his tears: "Kent, I'm not afraid to die. I trust completely in God. But I do hate to leave my wife and my children."

We wept and prayed together. Then Bill asked, "Why did you come in just now, at the very moment I needed someone with whom to share this pain? No one knew that I was here." I told him I just happened to be driving past the hospital and had this strong urging to stop to see if we had any patients there. I told him how I had resisted the urging but that it became so strong I had to stop. Again he got tears in his eyes and said, "God sent you didn't he! God knew I needed someone, and God sent you here at exactly the right time."

I visited and prayed with Bill several times over the next few months. On every visit he would remind me of that early morning call. Bill said that surprise visit had become a sign for him of God's love and concern and gave him great peace as he realized God was caring for him in such practical ways. Bill died about three months later with an incredible sense of acceptance, peace, and faith in the loving presence of God.

I do not think it was just a coincidence that I stopped by the hospital that day. If it had been up to me alone, I would not have stopped; I had other agenda on my mind. I believe it was the Spirit of God urging me from within to visit a person in need of empowerment.

I suspect you have had experiences similar to this one. God is always trying to give us guidance and empowerment if we will only listen. Have you ever had the experience of suddenly having someone come to mind whom you haven't thought about for a long time? Have you ever felt the urge to call someone or to write someone just out of the blue? Have you ever found a friend to listen to you describe your bad experience just when you needed one? Have you found renewed strength and hope during difficult moments? The Holy Spirit is always present, urging us to do those things that would bring joy and hope into the lives of others and empowering us with renewed strength and peace if we would only remain open and listen.

One of the major problems coaches have is that the players do not always heed the good advice the coach gives. Players sometimes do not listen well and want to do everything their own way. I suspect the Holy Spirit has the same problem with us. Good coaching is given by the Spirit, but we do not always listen well and we want to do everything our own way. For those who listen well and follow that inner voice, life is transformed and people are well served.

Pause for Reflection

When have you had experiences where you felt the Holy Spirit guiding you in some way?

When have you had ideas pop into your mind at the very time they were needed?

When have you happened to be at the right place at the right time for the encounter or experience you needed at that moment?

When have you met someone randomly who was able to help you in some important way?

When have you met someone randomly whom you were able to help in some important way?

We Believe in the Holy Spirit, God Present With Us for . . . Comfort and for Strength.

Fruits of the Spirit

Love

Joy

Peace

Patience

Kindness

Generosity

Faithfulness

Gentleness

Self-control

The Holy Spirit gives Christians comfort and strength in times of difficulty and tragedy. Recently, a woman shared with me the story of a terrible tragedy that occurred several years ago. On July 4, 1970, she and her family boarded her father-in-law's new boat for a ride on a lake. They were about fifty yards from shore when something went wrong; the boat suddenly began to sink. None of them were wearing life jackets. Her husband, father-in-law, and two-year-old daughter drowned. Meanwhile, the woman, who was six months pregnant, was trying to keep herself and her four-year-old son afloat. Eventually, another boat came by and rescued her and her son. Can you imagine the incredible grief and pain she went through as she attended funeral services for her husband, her daughter, and her father-in-law?

When the time came for the woman to deliver her baby, she went to the hospital petrified with fear. She was worried about the baby's well-being because of the physical and emotional trauma she had been through. She was still grieving and wanting so much to have her husband present as she gave birth to their third child.

The woman was lying in the delivery room rigid and tense, filled with fear and anxiety, when something happened. She felt a real presence in the room around her. Then she felt a gentle touching on her shoulders, but no human being was behind her. An incredible feeling of peace came over her, and she heard the words: "Everything's going to be OK." In that moment the woman relaxed and had a deep feeling of peace in her heart. She knew that her baby was going to be all right.

A beautiful baby girl was born almost immediately, perfectly healthy in every way. My friend concluded, "From that experience, I know God is real and God is present, seeking to give us the comfort and strength we need."

Pause for Reflection

When have you had an experience of the unseen presence of God giving you comfort and strength in a time of need?

Spirit of the Living God

Spirit of the living God,
    fall afresh on me.
Spirit of the living God,
    fall afresh on me.
Melt me, mold me,
    fill me, use me.
Spirit of the living God,
    fall afresh on me.

An Invitation to the Holy Spirit

O God, the Holy Spirit,
    come to us, and among us;
    come as the winds, and cleanse us;
    come as the fire, and burn;
    come as the dew, and refresh;
convict, convert, and consecrate
    many hearts and lives
      to our great good
      and to thy greater glory;
and this we ask for Jesus Christ's sake.
Amen.

Eric Milner-White. Used by permission of The Society for Promoting Christian Knowledge, London, England.

CHAPTER 4

GOD FORGIVES US

We believe in the forgiveness of sins,
in the life of love and prayer,
and in grace equal to every need.

"Pray then in this way:
Our Father in heaven,
  hallowed be your name.
  Your kingdom come.
  Your will be done,
    on earth as it is in heaven.
  Give us this day our daily bread.
  And forgive us our debts,
    as we also have forgiven our debtors.
  And do not bring us to the time of trial,
    but rescue us from the evil one.
For if you forgive others their trespasses, your
heavenly Father will also forgive you; but if you
do not forgive others, neither will your Father for-
give your trespasses."   (Matthew 6:9-15)

We Believe in the Forgiveness of Sins.

When I was a child, my father was a practic-ing alcoholic. Because of his drinking problem, he had a hard time keeping a job. We were always in financial difficulty. He was away from the family a lot; and when he was home, Dad would sometimes be verbally abusive. When he was not drinking, Dad was a wonderful person and realized how much damage his alcoholism caused. He tried to stop drinking many times on his own and would sometimes be successful for months at a time. Then he would think that he could take just one drink and that would be the end of his sobriety. Finally, my mother felt she could not endure the damage caused by his alcoholism any longer, so she filed for divorce.

Then, a miracle happened. My father con-tacted some members of Alcoholics Anonymous (AA). They began to share their experience in this program with him and how they were able to stay sober. Dad spent about a month living on a ranch with a member of Alcoholics Anony-mous and studying the twelve steps of AA.

The first step is confession, admitting that you are powerless over alcohol. The second step is to believe that there is a Power greater than yourself who can restore your sanity. When Dad confessed his powerlessness over alcohol, he had an experience of the presence of God in which he felt the reality of God's forgiveness for all the harm he had done in the past and God's strength to begin life anew. Dad went through the other steps of AA, in which he acknowl-

> **Sin:** The misuse of one's God-given free will
> (Genesis 3)
>
> **Grace:** God's love demonstrated in the death of Jesus Christ for the salvation of the world
> (John 3:16)

edged the pain he had caused others and made amends where possible. His life and the life of our family was transformed, and Dad never took another drink of alcohol.

Millions of people around the world have found new life through Alcoholics Anonymous or through one of the many other twelve-step programs that have sprung from it. All these programs are based on our need for confession and forgiveness. Regardless of our situation, renewal of life always begins with recognizing our sin, confessing it, and accepting God's forgiveness.

Seeking Forgiveness

At the heart of the Christian faith is the belief that we all sin and fall short of God's will for our lives. When we are honest with ourselves, we know we have not always kept our eyes focused on God. We have thought, said, and done things that displease God and that hurt others as well as ourselves. Christians are not people who think they are perfect. Christians are people who know that they are not perfect but that they can be forgiven. The church is not a haven for saints; it is a hospital for sinners.

When many people make a mistake, they try to hide it. Frequently, they seek someone else to blame for their mistakes. Everything is blamed on the environment or heredity or someone else, and therefore no one is personally responsible for his or her own sins and shortcomings. Christians are people who want:

> to "come clean,"
> to admit their own sins before God and others,
> to discover the wonderful cleansing power of forgiveness.

That is why Christians continually pray to God: "Forgive us our sins."

Pope John XXIII once went into a prison in Rome to preach to the prisoners. He gave a sermon on God's unconditional love and forgiveness. The Pope emphasized that no matter what people have done, God's love is so great that they can be forgiven and restored. All they have to do is acknowledge their sin and need for God.

After the Pope's message, a man who had committed murder came up to the Pope with tears in his eyes and asked, "Do you think God could even forgive me?" The Pope looked him lovingly in the face, reached out his big arms, and embraced the man as a sign of God's forgiveness and love. In a similar way, God is present in every moment with open arms to forgive and love us when we come to God and admit our sins and mistakes.

Pause for Reflection

Think about your life. What are the sins and shortcomings in your life that you have hidden or blamed on someone else?

What is keeping you from simply acknowledging your sins and asking God's forgiveness?

Offering Forgiveness to Others

Once we have been forgiven by God, we are called to offer that same forgiveness to others. In the Lord's Prayer we pray, "Forgive us our trespasses, as we forgive those who trespass against us." Jesus stressed that if we are not willing to forgive others, God's forgiveness cannot become real in our lives. God's outstretched arms offer forgiveness to us; but if we have folded our arms and closed our hearts, refusing to forgive others, then we cannot experience the reality of God's forgiveness in our lives.

The truth about life is that if we are not able to forgive others for the wrong things they have done to us, we are damaged. If we live with resentment and bitterness toward someone else, it is like a cancer within us, eating away our life and spirit. We must learn to forgive simply in order to live.

Several years ago in Hartford, Connecticut, two young men who were drunk got into a fight. One was shot and killed. Michael, the young man who killed him, was convicted of manslaughter and was sent to prison.

The young man who was killed was the son of a minister. At first, the minister was filled with anger and hatred toward the man who had killed his son; but he soon realized how those feelings were destroying him and his ministry. He had seen many people who were not able to forgive become consumed by their anger and hatred. He did not want that to happen to him. So he wrote Michael a letter telling him he had forgiven him for the love of God.

When Michael received the letter of forgiveness, tears ran down his cheeks. He had given up on life and was so discouraged he did not want to live any longer. But the minister's forgiveness gave him new hope, and they began to exchange letters. Eventually, the minister visited Michael in prison; and, at the end of the visit, they embraced and wept over the tragedy that had brought them together.

When Michael came before the parole board, the minister testified on his behalf. He helped Michael find a job when he got out of prison and performed his wedding ceremony about a year later. When asked how he could forgive and accept the man who had killed his son, the minister explained that he had to forgive Michael or his own hatred and anger would destroy him (story from *The Indianapolis Star*, November 12, 1994, pages 1 and 2).

" 'Teacher, which commandment in the law is the greatest?'
He [Jesus] said to him, ' "You shall love the Lord your God
with all your heart, and with all your soul, and with all your
mind." This is the greatest and first commandment. And a
second is like it: "You shall love your neighbor as yourself." ' "

(Matthew 22:36-39)

Pause for Reflection

Jesus was right. Unless we can forgive those who have hurt us, we cut off our own opportunity for forgiveness and life.

Who are the people who need your forgiveness?

Do you carry resentment or bitterness toward anyone?

How is that anger affecting your life?

When are you going to let the anger go?

We Believe . . . in the Life of Love and Prayer, and in Grace Equal to Every Need.

When Jesus was asked about the most important commandment of all, he said the most important commandment is to love. According to Jesus, loving appears to be more important than proper belief or following certain rituals. He did not mention those things in his response. Love is to be focused on God, on your neighbor, and on yourself; but the basic command is simply to be a loving person.

Lou was one of the most loving, prayerful, and grace-filled persons I have ever met. She was in her eighties when I first met her as a member of a congregation I served. Lou was absolutely in love with God and with every person she met. When the sun was shining, she was filled with praise to God for the beauty of sunny days. When it was raining or snowing, Lou praised God for the moisture or the beauty of snowflakes falling gently to the earth. When she was well, she praised God for good health. When she was sick, she praised God for God's healing power and the hospital personnel.

After church on Sundays, Lou would introduce herself to strangers, welcome them to the congregation, and express genuine interest in their lives. She especially loved children. They knew it and would flock around her at every chance.

Someone once said to me: "Lou must have

had an easy life to make her so full of love for God and everyone." I explained to him that the opposite was the case. Lou had had a very difficult life. Her first husband died of a heart attack, leaving her with five young children to raise. She worked her fingers to the bone in a variety of jobs—providing food, clothing, and shelter for her family—and insured that each of her children had a college education.

Later, Lou remarried. Her second husband, in a time of severe depression, committed suicide. In her later years, Lou fell and broke her hip. She was also slowly losing her eyesight. Lou had not lived an easy life.

One day I asked Lou how she kept such a positive and hopeful outlook in spite of the tragedies of her life. She explained that she began each day with this prayer of surrender: "Father, in your hands and keeping now I place all my affairs, all my many situations, all my hopes, all my cares, all my loved ones, fully knowing they can neither fail nor fall when they follow your direction; for your love surrounds us all."

In surrendering herself and her loved ones into God's hands, Lou was expressing her love and trust in God. She had discovered that God's grace is sufficient to every need. Because Lou was so surrendered to God, God's love flowed into her and through her into the lives of others.

The Supreme Example

Jesus is the ultimate model of one who lived a life of love and prayer and demonstrated that God's grace is equal to every need. He expressed his love for all people by associating with tax collectors, prostitutes, and other sinners. He demonstrated God's unconditional love by forgiving a woman taken in adultery (John 8:1-11) and by telling a story with a hated Samaritan as the hero (Luke 10:25-37).

The Gospels also tell us that Jesus often went out alone to pray. "In the morning, while it was still very dark, he [Jesus] got up and went out to a deserted place, and there he prayed" (Mark 1:35). On the last night of his life on earth, Jesus knelt and prayed a prayer of absolute surrender in the Garden of Gethsemane: "Father, if you are willing, remove this cup from me; yet, not my will but yours be done" (Luke 22:42).

Even though Jesus lost his life on a cross, he discovered God's grace was sufficient to

carry him through death to resurrection. The same thing is true for us: When we surrender ourselves totally into the hands of God, we find that God carries us through the crucifying experiences of life into new life. God's grace is equal to every need.

Pause for Reflection

A life of love and prayer is a life of total surrender in which we discover for ourselves that God's grace is sufficient for every need. One of the reasons we fail to discover that God's grace is sufficient is because we have never abandoned ourselves totally into God's hands.

Why is it so difficult to surrender oneself and one's loved ones into the hands of God?

What keeps you from loving God enough to trust God with all your concerns?

Why do you feel the need to control your life?

What would surrendering your concerns mean for your life?

Amazing Grace

Amazing grace! How sweet the sound
 that saved a wretch like me!
I once was lost, but now am found;
 was blind, but now I see.

'Twas grace that taught my heart to fear,
 and grace my fears relieved;
how precious did that grace appear
 the hour I first believed.

Through many dangers, toils, and
 snares,
 I have already come;
'tis grace hath brought me safe thus far,
 and grace will lead me home.

The Lord has promised good to me,
 his word my hope secures;
he will my shield and portion be,
 as long as life endures.

John Newton

Prayer of Confession

Almighty and merciful God,
 we know that when we offend another, we offend you.
We are aware that we have often allowed the shadow of hate
 to cloud our souls, hiding the light from our unseeking eyes.
We have said unpleasant and hurtful things to our brothers and sisters
 when they failed to live up to our expectations.
Grant that we might find that spark of love that ever burns within us,
 the love that you have shown to us even when we failed you.
Fan the embers of that love until it roars again
 in flames of love, peace, and reconciliation.
Forgive us our sins
 and help us to forgive those who have sinned against us.
Lead us into new life through your Son Jesus Christ,
 who died for the sins of all. Amen.

Michael J. O'Donnell, from *The United Methodist Book of Worship,* No. 481; © 1992 The United Methodist Publishing House.

CHAPTER 5

GOD INSTRUCTS US

We believe in the Word of God contained in the Old and New Testaments as the sufficient rule both of faith and of practice.

"But as for you, continue in what you have learned and firmly believed, knowing from whom you learned it, and how from childhood you have known the sacred writings that are able to instruct you for salvation through faith in Christ Jesus. All scripture is inspired by God and is useful for teaching, for reproof, for correction, and for training in righteousness, so that everyone who belongs to God may be proficient, equipped for every good work." (2 Timothy 3:14-17)

"Now Jesus did many other signs in the presence of his disciples, which are not written in this book. But these are written so that you may come to believe that Jesus is the Messiah, the Son of God, and that through believing you may have life in his name." (John 20:30-31)

We Believe in the Word of God . . . as the Sufficient Rule Both of Faith and of Practice.

Several years ago a man named Jackson Brown wanted to give his son, Adam, some words of counsel and advice as Adam went away for his first year of college. Mr. Brown said he believed it was not the responsibility of parents to pave the road for their children but to provide them with a road map to help them find their way through life. Jackson Brown began to collect and compose some brief "words of wisdom" that he felt his son might find helpful on his life journey. He put them in a binder to give to his son at the appropriate time.

After Jackson Brown and his wife helped Adam settle into his dorm room for his first year at college, Jackson took his son aside and gave him the notebook. He told his son, "This is what I know about living a happy and rewarding life, and I want to share it with you."

Adam received the notebook as the very special gift it was and thanked and hugged his father. A few days later, Adam called his dad and said, "Dad, I've been reading the instruction book; and I think it's one of the best gifts I've ever received. I'm going to add to it and someday give it to my son."

Later, Jackson Brown published those notes to his son under the title *Life's Little Instruction Book* (Rutledge Hill Press, 1991) with the subtitle, "511 suggestions, observations, and reminders on how to live a happy and rewarding life." This little book is simply filled with

Life's Little Instruction Book

511 suggestions, observations, and reminders on how to live a happy and rewarding life

Compliment three people every day.

Watch a sunrise at least once a year.

Remember other people's birthdays.

Overtip breakfast waitresses.

Have a firm handshake.

Be forgiving of yourself and others.

Learn three clean jokes.

Never give up on anybody. Miracles happen every day.

brief words of wisdom and advice for living an effective and meaningful life.

In many ways the Bible is like *Life's Little Instruction Book* because they both have the same purpose—to help us live meaningful and joyful lives. Like a loving parent, God did not send us out into the world without an instruction book. God did not pave the road of life for us and make life easy, but God did give us a guidebook and road map for the journey.

God's Guidebook

Christians believe Scripture is God's "Big Instruction Book" to teach us how to live a meaningful, joyful life that makes a difference in the world. However, our problem is that many of us have not read God's instruction manual for life or we read it only infrequently or we do not follow it very well. We often treat Scripture like those little instruction sheets that come with the toys we give our children for birthdays and Christmas.

On our grandson's birthday we gave him one of those big plastic jungle gym sets that come in a box that says, "Some assembly required." That was an understatement. It looked simple enough, so I just began to put things together according to the picture on the box. I soon found that something was seriously wrong, however. The jungle gym set was wobbly and did not stand up straight. About that time, my wife gently handed me the instruction manual. Since I was desperate, I began to read it. I discovered, when I read the instruction manual, that the jungle gym set was not as hard to put together as I was making it.

God has given us life and an instruction manual to go with it, but many of us do not think we need it. We think we can figure life out by ourselves. We do not feel a need to listen to God or anyone else. However, often there comes a time in our lives when we have thoroughly messed things up. We have lost our self-esteem and gone through one broken relationship after another, or we have experienced some tragedy in our lives. Only then do we become desperate enough to be willing to read and apply God's instruction book for our lives.

Pause for Reflection

During the Vietnam War, many American soldiers and airmen were taken captive by the North Vietnamese and held in a prisoner of war camp in Hanoi. They were often tortured, beaten, denied food, and isolated from one another to try to break their spirits. The men discovered they could communicate with one another by writing notes on slips of paper and passing them from cell to cell.

Some of the prisoners began to write verses of Scripture they could remember as words of encouragement to one another. Someone remembered the verses of the Twenty-third Psalm. Someone else wrote the words of the Lord's Prayer. Another person remembered John 3:16. Others wrote scattered verses from the Bible as they could remember them. When one of the prisoners would come back from being beaten or tortured during interrogation or when they heard a prisoner crying out that he could not take it anymore, they would send their little slips of paper with Scripture verses on them to the person in need.

One of the ways these men could express their concern for one another was to share their verses of faith and hope from the Scriptures. They did not have much of the Bible, but they had enough to get them through the rough places of life. After they were released, many of the former POW's said those few verses of Scripture that they would read over and over enabled them to keep going during months and even years of confinement and torture.

The prisoners of war did not have much of the Bible, but they had enough to get them through a rough time of life. Do you have enough of the Bible in you to get you through the rough places in your life? Why or why not?

When you see someone in pain, do you have any life-giving verses to share with them? List some verses below.

Understanding the Bible

One of the frequent objections to studying the Bible is: "I can't understand it." When some people try to read the Scriptures, much of the content does not make sense to them; so they give up on it.

The Bible:

—contains sixty-six books (thirty-nine in the Old Testament and twenty-seven in the New Testament)

—was written over a one thousand-year period by many different authors.

—contains different types of literature: laws, history, poetry, philosophy, prophetic writings, gospels, letters, apocalypses.

We need to understand the historical setting and context of a passage to comprehend what

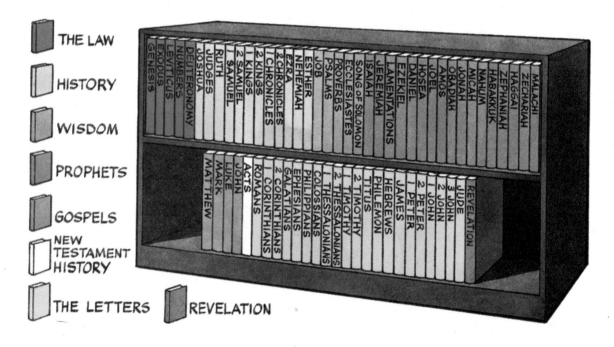

it meant when it was first written and what it might mean for us today. Many helps are available—concordances, commentaries, Bible dictionaries, Bible surveys, in-depth study materials, study classes.

Parts of the Bible are difficult to understand, and much detailed study may be necessary. However, as Mark Twain once said, "It's not the parts of the Bible I don't understand that bother me; it's the parts of the Bible I do understand."

Pause for Reflection

Jesus said:

"You shall love the Lord your God with all your heart, and with all your soul, and with all your mind, and with all your strength," and "You shall love your neighbor as yourself" (Mark 12:30).

"Love your enemies and pray for those who persecute you" (Matthew 5:44).

"Those who want to save their life will lose it" (Mark 8:35).

"If anyone strikes you on the cheek, offer the other also" (Luke 6:29).

Forgive "not seven times, but, I tell you, seventy-seven times" (Matthew 18:21-22).

"As you did it to one of the least of these who are members of my family, you did it to me" (Matthew 25:40).

"Do to others as you would have them do to you" (Luke 6:31).

We have a fairly good idea about what Jesus is calling us to do in passages like these. Our problem is that we pretend not to understand so we do not have to do it. What are you pretending not to know about the message of the Bible?

How might you respond differently to the message?

SHAPED BY THE WORD

The Scriptures are exceedingly relevant to my daily life. Every morning I read a devotional guide entitled *A Guide for Prayer for All God's People* by Rueben Job and Norman Shawchuck (Upper Room Books, 1994). Each day's devotion contains an opening prayer, suggested Scripture readings, quotations by various authors, a time for reflection and prayer, a hymn, and a benediction. It's amazing to me how frequently the texts and reflections for the day provide guidance for the issues I face that day.

One day I was given a particular award, and I felt proud about receiving this special recognition. The next morning I opened the Bible to the suggested text and read these words from Paul's letter to the Romans: "I say to everyone among you not to think of yourself more highly than you ought to think, but to think with sober judgment, each according to the measure of faith that God has assigned" (Romans 12:3). I was thinking "more highly of myself than I ought to think." These words of Scripture humbled me and made me realize how my pride often gets in the way of my desire to serve God with my whole being. Have there been times when particular words of Scripture have been the precise words you needed to hear at a certain moment in your life?

Robert Mulholland, in his book *Shaped by the Word* (The Upper Room, 1985), points out that we should open ourselves so much to the Scriptures that we are literally "shaped" by the Word of God contained in the Bible. When we allow God to transform us through the Scriptures, our thoughts, feelings, and actions are all shaped and influenced by the words of the Bible.

One of the ways Mulholland suggests studying Scripture is to imagine yourself in a particular story. Once I attended a workshop in which the leader invited us to imagine we were at the scene when the Pharisees dragged a woman taken in adultery before Jesus (John 8:1-11). The leader asked us to close our eyes and to become quiet and then to allow ourselves simply to appear in the story and hear what God might say to us.

During the first reading of the story, I simply showed up in the crowd and watched as the Pharisees dragged the woman through the streets, threw her down at the feet of Jesus, and prepared to stone her to death. I waited with the crowd as Jesus paused before saying to the Pharisees: "Let anyone among you who is without sin be the first to throw a stone at her." I watched as Jesus took the woman by the hand, lifted her up, and said: "Neither do I condemn you. Go your way, and from now on do not sin again." I experienced a wonderful feeling of love and appreciation for Jesus because of his incredible wisdom and compassion. When the Pharisees came pointing out the woman's sin, he turned it around and caused them to look at their sin. Jesus did not condone what she did; he simply forgave her and invited her to begin a new life. I certainly never would have had the insight and wisdom to answer the Pharisees in such a way.

The second time our leader read the story, I suddenly found myself as a Pharisee. I did not want to be a Pharisee, but in my imagination I saw myself dragging someone through the streets to Jesus. I looked down to see who I was dragging, and it was my son. I found myself throwing him down at the feet of Jesus and saying, "This young man has been caught in the act of denting his father's car. Such people are to be condemned." A few weeks earlier,

our son had dented our car accidentally; and this was exactly the judgmental attitude I had expressed toward him.

Then Jesus looked at me and said: "Let anyone among you who is without sin be the first to throw a stone." I remembered my own accidents with the car in the past; and my self-righteous, judgmental attitude toward my son melted away. I realized how often I can be judgmental and self-righteous toward others rather than seeing my own sins and shortcomings.

The third time the leader read the story I appeared as the person being dragged through the streets. I wondered, *What have I done wrong?* I looked up and saw that I was being dragged by two fellow pastors. When they got me to Jesus, they threw me down and said, "This man has been caught in the act of being a workaholic. Such people are to be condemned." It

felt so painful because I knew their accusation was true. My persistent sin is working too hard and neglecting myself and my family.

Then Jesus looked at those other ministers and said, "Let anyone among you who is without sin be the first to throw a stone." They dropped their stones and went away; and Jesus picked me up saying, "Neither do I condemn you. Go your way, and from now on do not sin." Jesus did not condone my behavior, but he forgave me for it. This powerful encounter with the living Christ in Scripture caused me to reevaluate my life and to make some significant changes.

One of the most significant ways we encounter the living Christ is through the stories in the Gospels. When you open yourself to them, you too may discover a profound, life-changing personal word.

Pause for Reflection

I once heard it said that a person who can read and does not is no better off than a person who is illiterate and cannot read at all. If we can read the Bible but do not, we make ourselves illiterate to the Word of God contained in Scripture and closed to the power and wisdom God has given us for our lives.

When is the best time for you to read and ponder the Scriptures?

Will you join a Bible study group to help you grow in your faith? Why or why not?

A Final Word

God has given us an instruction book for life, but it does us no good if it remains on the bookshelf unread. Christians are people who not only say they believe in the Word of God contained in the Old and New Testaments but people who also actually read the Scriptures and encounter the living God through the Old and New Testaments.

O Word of God Incarnate

O Word of God incarnate, O Wisdom from on high,
  O Truth unchanged, unchanging, O Light of our dark sky:
we praise you for the radiance that from the hallowed page,
  a lantern to our footsteps, shines on from age to age.

The church from you, our Savior, received the gift divine,
  and still that light is lifted o'er all the earth to shine.
It is the sacred vessel where gems of truth are stored;
  it is the heaven-drawn picture of Christ, the living Word.

The Scripture is a banner before God's host unfurled;
  it is a shining beacon above the darkling world.
It is the chart and compass that o'er life's surging tide,
  mid mists and rocks and quicksands, to you, O Christ, will guide.

O make your church, dear Savior, a lamp of purest gold,
  to bear before the nations your true light as of old.
O teach your wandering pilgrims by this their path to trace,
  till, clouds and darkness ended, they see you face to face.

William W. How

Concerning the Scriptures

  Blessed Lord, you have caused all holy Scriptures to be
written for our learning. Grant us so to hear them, read,
mark, learn, and inwardly digest them, that we may
embrace and ever hold fast the blessed hope of everlasting
life, which you have given us in our Savior Jesus Christ,
who lives and reigns with you and the Holy Spirit, One
God, forever and ever. Amen.

After The Book of Common Prayer

CHAPTER 6

GOD CALLS AND SENDS US

We believe in the church,
those who are united in the living Lord
for the purpose of worship and service.
We believe in the reign of God
as the divine will realized in human
society,
and in the family of God,
where we are all brothers and sisters.

"Now when Jesus came into the district of Caesarea Philippi, he asked his disciples, 'Who do people say that the Son of Man is?' And they said, 'Some say John the Baptist, but others Elijah, and still others Jeremiah or one of the prophets.' He said to them, 'But who do you say that I am?' Simon Peter answered, 'You are the Messiah, the Son of the living God.' And Jesus answered him, 'Blessed are you, Simon son of Jonah! For flesh and blood has not revealed this to you, but my Father in heaven. And I tell you, you are Peter, and on this rock I will build my church, and the gates of Hades will not prevail against it.' "

(Matthew 16:13-18)

We Believe in the Church.

When I was a child, our family did not go to church. My parents, two sisters, and I lived in a one-room apartment in the back of a cafe, where Mother worked as a waitress. Dad was an alcoholic, could not hold a job, and was gone a lot. After he joined Alcoholics Anonymous, however, our lives were transformed. He was able to hold a job, we moved out of the one-room apartment into a house, and Dad insisted that we start attending a church. The basic reason he wanted us to attend church was to say "thank you" to God for saving him and our family.

I remember standing with my family in the front of a small sanctuary when I was twelve years old and being received as new members in that congregation. A year earlier, I was ashamed to be seen in public with my dad because of his alcoholism. Now I felt proud to stand beside him because of what God had done in our lives. At the end of that worship service, all forty people in attendance hugged us and welcomed us into the fellowship of the church. I remember having tears in my eyes because it felt so good to be loved and accepted by this Christian fellowship.

This experience led our family to love the church and to attend regularly. Later, I became active in the youth fellowship group. While attending a church camp, I felt the call to ordained ministry. Consequently, it is easy for me to say, "I believe in the church," because a congregation of Christians helped God heal our family by their love and acceptance.

Pause for Reflection

What is your earliest memory of the church?

When have you felt accepted by the church? Why?

When have you felt rejected by the church? Why?

The Church's Beginning

When Jesus came into the world, he did not simply give his teachings to one person to pass on to another. No, he called a group of people together who would live and share their lives in community with him for three years. In this group they would not only hear about his teachings; they would also live them together. Here Jesus talked about the nature of God; told stories to help them remember; and demonstrated faith, forgiveness, and unconditional love. The Gospels are filled with stories about Jesus and his disciples (a group), not Jesus and his disciple (an individual).

On one occasion, Jesus and his disciples went on a retreat to Caesarea Philippi, away from the crowds. Jesus asked the disciples: "Who do people say that the Son of Man is?" They answered, "Some say John the Baptist, but others Elijah, and still others Jeremiah or one of the prophets." Jesus said to them: "But who do you say that I am?" And Peter, speaking what was in the heart of all the disciples, said: "You are the Messiah, the Son of the living God." Jesus responded, "Blessed are you, Simon son of Jonah! For flesh and blood has not revealed this to you, but my Father in heaven. And I tell you, you are Peter, and on this rock I will build my church, and the gates of Hades will not prevail against it." (See Matthew 16:13-18.)

What was the "rock" on which Jesus would build his church?

Some say the "rock" was Peter himself.

Others say the "rock" was Peter's confession of faith in Jesus as the Messiah.

Still others say the disciples as a group were the "rock" on which Jesus would build his church.

Paul, for example, emphasized the important role of all the disciples in building the church when he wrote to the Christians at Ephesus: "You are citizens with the saints and also members of the household of God, built upon the foundation of the apostles and prophets, with Christ Jesus himself as the cornerstone" (Ephesians 2:19-20).

After Jesus' death and resurrection, the disciples stayed together as a group. While they were praying together, the Holy Spirit descended on them with power; and the church as a fellowship of witness and service became a living reality in the world. (See Acts 2.)

Pause for Reflection

While each person must make an individual decision to follow Jesus Christ, once that decision is made, Christ calls us to be part of a group of followers called the church. Sometimes, people will say: "I believe in God or I believe in Jesus, but I don't believe in the church or I can be just as good a Christian without the church." Jesus, apparently, did not believe that his followers should travel through this life alone because he called them to be part of a group traveling together, not just a series of individuals who travel alone in the same direction.

Paul believed in the group nature of the Christian journey because he compared the church to the human body. It would make no more sense to believe that a Christian could travel life's journey alone than it would to say that the eye, the ear, the hand, or the foot could live and carry out its function apart from the rest of the body. (See 1 Corinthians 12.)

How would you respond if someone said he or she did not need to be part of a church to be a follower of Jesus Christ?

To Be or Not to Be?

A pastor once told me about a member of his church who came to see him to tell him that he did not want to be a member of the church anymore. The man explained that he liked to watch religious programs on television every Sunday morning with their outstanding music and preaching. He felt he could get his religious inspiration and growth through these television ministries. So the man asked to have his name removed from the church roll.

A few months later, the man had a massive heart attack and was rushed to a hospital. His wife called the pastor, who went to the hospital and prayed with the family for the man's life. All night long the man hung on that thin line between life and death. He lived, and during his days of recovery people from the church stopped by to visit and pray with him and sent flowers and cards. The church members surrounded this man and his family with love and support during their time of crisis.

A few weeks later the man said to the pastor: "I guess I was wrong. When I had my heart attack, the television preacher did not come to the hospital to pray for me; and the congregation I saw on television did not stop by to visit me. I guess I do need the church. Will you put my name back on the membership roll?"

Sometimes we think we can complete life's journey successfully on our own or with a little help from a television program. God, however, calls us to be part of a fellowship of believers who love, encourage, and challenge us to grow and who help us experience God's unconditional love in community.

Pause for Reflection

Our journey through life as a group of Christians is similar to the migratory habits of geese. Every fall thousands of geese migrate from Canada to the southern parts of the United States for the winter, just like some people do. Geese, however, always fly together in a V-formation. Wildlife biologists studied this phenomenon and discovered that geese can fly about 60 percent farther and stay up in the air longer by flying together than by flying alone. Flying together in that V-formation, each goose provides additional lift for the goose behind, and they can all fly farther and longer. The geese in the back always honk to encourage the lead goose, who has no one in front of him or her providing additional lift. When the lead goose tires out, he or she goes to the end of the line and another goose takes over. If one of the geese is injured or sick and unable to go on, two or three

Ron Sanford/© Tony Stone Worldwide

other geese drop out and stay with that goose until it either dies or is able to fly again.

In a similar way Christians have discovered that it is better to travel through this life together in groups than to try to travel alone. Like the geese, we provide lift and encouragement for one another in our life journeys as we pray for one another, listen to one another, and laugh and cry together. We are also called to provide words of encouragement for our leaders and to take our turn in leadership responsibilities. Furthermore, when one of our number is injured or sick, we stay with him or her, providing companionship, love, and support in his or her time of need. Christ called the first disciples to embody the Christian life together as a group, and he calls followers today to journey together.

How do you experience "lift" or encouragement in your congregation?

How do you encourage your leaders?

How do you "take your turn" in leadership responsibilities?

Do you visit those in your fellowship who are injured or sick? Why or why not?

I once served a church where there was a sign that could be read on the way into the sanctuary: "ENTER TO WORSHIP." The back of the sign, which could be read as one left the church, said: "DEPART TO SERVE." We enter the church to say "Thank you, God" for the gift of life itself with all its joys and challenges; and then, as renewed and inspired people, we depart to share God's unconditional love with others.

Human beings are given two legs on which to walk through life's journey. As Christians, the worship of God and the service of others are the two legs on which we walk through our Christian journey. If we try to worship without serving or serve without worshiping, we disable ourselves and cannot fulfill God's vision for our life journey.

Jesus emphasized the importance of worship and service when he told his disciples that the

The Sacraments

Christians participate in the Sacraments of the church initiated by Jesus Christ:

Holy Communion—an act of worship in which bread and wine are consumed in thankfulness for and remembrance of the sacrifice of the body and blood of Jesus Christ for the salvation of the world.
(See Luke 22:14-20.)

Baptism—an act of worship in which water is used to symbolize one's cleansing from sin and adoption by God's grace into the community of Christians.
(See Matthew 3:13-17.)

We Believe in the Church...for the Purpose of Worship and Service.

We Believe in the Reign of God . . . and in the Family of God.

greatest commandment is to love God with our whole being and to love our neighbors as ourselves (Matthew 22:34-40). We express our love for God and our thankfulness for all God has done for us in worship; and we express our love for our neighbors through our acts of loving service.

A widespread contemporary movement encourages people to "PRACTICE RANDOM KINDNESS AND SENSELESS ACTS OF BEAUTY." In our society we have seen much random violence and countless senseless acts of destruction. Regularly, there are news reports of drive-by shootings or shootings into large groups of people. Persons are killed randomly simply because they happen to be in the wrong place at the wrong time. In the 1995 bombing of the federal building in Oklahoma City, 168 people were killed simply because they happened to work or be doing business in that building at the time the bomb went off. Every random act of violence contributes to the large black cloud of despair and cynicism that hangs over humanity and that pervades much of our contemporary society.

What can we do? God can use us to overcome these random acts of violence by practicing random acts of kindness. While some people injure or kill people they do not even know, we can love and assist people we do not even know. Every random act of kindness sends a beam of light into the cloud of darkness. When enough people begin to treat strangers with kindness rather than indifference or violence, we will begin to see a transformation in society in which God's reign is being realized and in which we all recognize that we are brothers and sisters in the family of God.

During Random Acts of Kindness Week, a member of our congregation decided to purchase two dozen roses, to visit a nursing home at random, and to give the roses to residents. After receiving permission from the person in charge, he began to walk up and down the halls visiting with residents and leaving them a rose.

The man said he left that nursing home with tears running down his cheeks and with a deep sense of gratitude that God had used him to bring joy to persons in that particular nursing home on that particular day.

Random acts of kindness are not done to receive recognition or credit but to share love and concern with others and in doing so to provide light and hope in the midst of darkness. Wherever this kind of love is expressed, we see practical expressions of God's will being realized in human society.

Random Acts of Kindness

I may have a brilliant mind, a wonderful personality, and a healthy body;
but if I am not kind to those around me,
it does me no good.

I may have a good income, a beautiful home, and an expensive car;
but if I am not kind and generous in sharing them,
I don't make a difference in the world.

I may have great success in my business or profession; I may have power and influence over many people;
but if I don't treat people with kindness,
I am a failure.

Kindness is love in action.
Kindness is the pebble in the pond, whose ripples can change the world.

Having the faith to move mountains is great.
Having hope in bleak circumstances is wonderful.
But deeds of loving kindness transform lives and last forever.
I may have many wonderful qualities in my life,
but without kindness they are not enough.

Pause for Reflection

When have you practiced random acts of kindness?

Have you ever experienced random acts of kindness from someone you did not know?

What difference do you think it would make toward realizing God's reign in the world if everyone practiced random kindness and senseless acts of beauty?

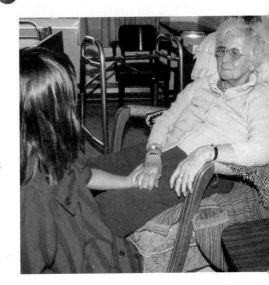

Final Judgment

In Matthew 25:31-46, Jesus tells a story about the Final Judgment in which persons are assessed on the way they have treated one another. To one group he says, "Come, you that are blessed by my Father, . . . for I was hungry and you gave me food, I was thirsty and you gave me something to drink, I was a stranger and you welcomed me, I was naked and you gave me clothing, I was sick and you took care of me, I was in prison and you visited me." The righteous are surprised and ask the Lord when they have done these acts of kindness to him. The Lord responds: "Truly, I tell you, just as you did it to one of the least of these who are members of my family, you did it to me."

A second group of persons are condemned at the Final Judgment because they failed to do acts of kindness to strangers in need. Jesus makes it abundantly clear that the reign of God in this world is realized when people reach out in loving care for others and treat one another as brothers and sisters in the family of God.

The reign of God in the world involves not only individual acts of kindness and service but also corporate acts of justice and mercy for all people. Sometimes persons in our society are looked down upon because of their race, creed, sex, age, national origin, or disability. Jesus saw every person as a precious child of God, who is made in the image of God and who should be loved and affirmed as unique and irreplaceable.

Martin Luther King, Jr., gave his life to help realize the just reign of God in human society. At a time when millions of persons of color were being legally discriminated against because of the color of their skin, Dr. King led a civil rights movement that helped pass laws giving all persons in American society an equal opportunity to learn, to work, and to live. Unfortunately, growing numbers of groups still preach hate toward persons who are different from themselves rather than seeing all persons as brothers and sisters in the family of God.

Jesus was an open person who included the outcast, the prostitute, and other sinners in his circle of love and who stood against those in his society who would exclude others from God's family. In a similar way, being faithful to Christ today involves us standing up for the inclusion of all persons in God's circle of unconditional love.

In August, 1962, Dr. King gave a speech in front of thousands of people at the Lincoln Memorial in Washington, DC, in which he said: "I have a dream that my four little children will

"At our local department store, an elderly gentleman wih a walker was attempting to exchange several purchases when the clerk told him he was $18 short. The woman next to him opened her handbag, took out a $20 bill, laid it on the counter, and hurried out of the store. Beautiful! Rusty in Northridge, California" (Ann Landers column, May 20, 1995. © Creators Syndicate).

"Recently, we stopped to have dinner in a restaurant when some other diners overheard our conversation in which we mentioned we had just given birth to quadruplet boys. Without our knowledge, these wonderful people paid for our dinner and left the message that we probably needed to save as much money as possible. In this world of terrorism, domestic violence, murder, etc., it is incredibly encouraging to see that there are still just plain nice people for our new sons to grow up around. Whoever you may be, this is a thank you six times over for your unselfish act of generosity. Kokomo, Indiana" (Letter to the Editor, *The Indianapolis Star*, May 20, 1995).

one day live in a nation where they will not be judged by the color of their skin but by the content of their character.

"I have a dream today [that] all of God's children, black . . . and white . . . , Jews and Gentiles, Protestants and Catholics, will be able to join hands and sing . . . 'Free at last! Free at last! Thank God almighty, we are free at last!' " That dream has not yet been fully realized, but Christians are those who live and work to make that dream a reality.

We Are the Church

The church is not a building,
  the church is not a steeple,
the church is not a resting place,
  the church is a people.

Refrain:
I am the church!
  You are the church!
We are the church together!
All who follow Jesus,
  all around the world!
Yes, we're the church together!

We're many kinds of people,
  with many kinds of faces,
all colors and all ages, too,
  from all times and places.

Refrain

Sometimes the church is marching,
  sometimes it's bravely burning,
sometimes it's riding, sometimes hiding,
  always it's learning.

Refrain

And when the people gather,
  there's singing and there's praying,
there's laughing and there's crying
    sometimes,
  all of it saying:

Refrain

Richard K. Avery and Donald S. Marsh. Copyright © 1972 by Hope Publishing Co., Carol Stream, IL 60188.

For the Unity of Christ's Body
Help each of us, gracious God,
  to live in such magnanimity and restraint
that the Head of the church may never have
    cause to say to any one of us,
  "This is my body, broken by you." Amen.

Chinese Prayer

CHAPTER 7

GOD GIVES US VICTORY

© 1994 Comstock, Inc.

We believe in the final triumph of righteousness
and in the life everlasting.

"It was now about noon, and darkness came over the whole land until three in the afternoon, while the sun's light failed; and the curtain of the temple was torn in two. Then Jesus, crying with a loud voice, said, 'Father, into your hands I commend my spirit.' Having said this, he breathed his last."

(Luke 23:44-46)

"But on the first day of the week, at early dawn, they came to the tomb, taking the spices that they had prepared. They found the stone rolled away from the tomb, but when they went in, they did not find the body. While they were perplexed about this, suddenly two men in dazzling clothes stood beside them. The women were terrified and bowed their faces to the ground, but the men said to them, 'Why do you look for the living among the dead? He is not here, but has risen.' "

(Luke 24:1-5)

We Believe in the Final Triumph of Righteousness.

A woman shared some of the tragedies in her life with me. During the past year she had gone through a divorce she did not want, her father's death, the loss of a job she loved, and the discovery of a lump in her breast. She was fearful that she might require surgery. Through her tears she said: "It's just not fair. Why are all these terrible things happening to me? I don't deserve all this." She was right; life is just not fair. She did not deserve all her heartache.

I affirmed her feelings and then began to tell her about someone else who experienced the unfairness of life. I told her about Jesus, who knew just how she felt because he too went through one tragedy after another that he did not deserve. Jesus lived a good life; he went about healing the sick, the lepers, and the blind. He accepted those who were untouchable and unwanted by society; he told them about the unconditional love of God for all people. Jesus demonstrated God's acceptance by sitting down at the dinner table and breaking bread with people who were looked down upon. Whatever else you may believe about Jesus, it is obvious that he was a good man who went about doing acts of kindness and mercy for others.

Jesus did not deserve all the tragedy that happened to him. When he was just thirty-three years old, he was betrayed into the hands of his enemies by one of his best friends. He was abandoned by his other friends. He was whipped with a Roman lash, and he was nailed to a cross where he hung for six agonizing hours before he died. Life was not fair to Jesus. He did not deserve all that pain and suffering. He lived a good life and what did he get? He was crucified.

The truth about life is that life is not fair. Jesus knew it and we know it. Challenges, sufferings, disappointments, and heartaches come into every life because life is not fair. I have never met anyone who has gotten through life without some pain and tragedy.

Many people think Michael Jordan has it made. He is one of the most popular sports figures in the world; he has incredible ability on the basketball court; and he makes millions of dollars advertising various products. Yet Michael, in spite of his talent, his wealth, and his fame has not been spared from tragedy.

Michael Jordan had a tremendous relationship with his father, who was his number one fan. When he played basketball, Michael always knew his father was watching him, either in the stands or on television. After every game they would talk about the plays by phone. His father was a great source of encouragement and hope to Michael and probably the person Michael loved most.

To express his love and appreciation for his father, Michael bought him an expensive new car. One day the elder Mr. Jordan was taking a trip in his new car. A couple of young men saw this elderly man in his big expensive car, followed him for a while, stopped him, beat him to death, and stole the car.

Michael Jordan's heart was broken. The enthusiasm for playing basketball went out of him, since his father was not there to watch him and to cheer him on. He retired from the Chicago Bulls at the height of his career and then tried to play professional baseball. That did not work well because Michael was still recovering from the grief and pain of his father's death. Eventually, Michael returned to professional basketball and once again electrified audiences with his incredible talent and skill.

Michael Jordan's wealth, fame, and ability did not protect him from the tragedies of life. Everyone discovers that tragic things happen in life and that no one is immune to them.

Pause for Reflection

Who are some of the people you know who have suffered tragedy and heartache in their lives?

When have you felt that life is not fair?

What disappointments have you experienced in your life?

God Is Good

Life is not fair, but God is good. In spite of the difficulties and tragedies that come to us in life, God is always present to bring new life and hope. Like Jesus, all of us go through crucifying times in our lives; but God is always with us to bring about a resurrection in our lives.

According to Luke's Gospel, early on the Sunday morning after the Crucifixion, some women came to the tomb where Jesus had been buried. They found the stone rolled away, so they went into the tomb but did not find his body there. Suddenly, two angels appeared to them and said, "Why do you look for the living among the dead? He is not here, but has risen." Later on that day the women experienced his risen presence.

While the Gospel writers have different details about how many people went to the tomb on that first Easter morning and when and where Jesus appeared to them, they are united in the affirmation that out of this crucifying experience in Jesus' life, God brought a resurrection and new life.

The good news is that even though life was not fair to Jesus and it is not fair to us, God is always working to lead us through every tragedy into new life. While it may often appear that evil and hatred are in control, Christians believe "in the final triumph of righteousness." We believe that no matter how great the suffering, God will have the last word and that word will be one of life and love.

On Palm Sunday, 1994, a rapidly moving tornado passed through Piedmont, Alabama, and destroyed the Goshen United Methodist Church while the congregation was attending worship.

Sonia Halliday Photographs

© Gene Moore/PHOTOTAKE

With little warning, the walls of the church building collapsed, the roof fell in, ninety people were injured, and twenty people were killed. Half of those killed were children. Kelly Clem, pastor of the church, discovered that her four-year-old daughter, Hannah, was among the dead.

When a tragedy like this happens, we have to admit that life is not fair. It is not fair that these little children should lose their lives so tragically or that other people should lose their loved ones in this natural disaster.

But that was not the end of the story for Goshen United Methodist Church. One year after the tornado destroyed their building, the people of the church gathered in an open field about a quarter of a mile from the site of the destroyed building for a groundbreaking ceremony for their new church facility. As part of the service, Rev. Clem explained to the congregation that they would build the new church in the shape of a butterfly because the butterfly is a symbol of new life and resurrection.

Because of what the tornado had done, the congregation had been through crucifixion. They knew all about suffering, death, and heartache. In the past year, however, they had experienced resurrection in the generous outpouring of gifts and prayers from people all around the world. They had experienced resurrection in feeling the hand of God carrying them through their losses. They had also experienced resurrection as they felt a deeper love for one another. Out of their terrible crucifying experience God was working to bring about new life for all of them.

At the end of the groundbreaking service, Rev. Clem asked everyone to write messages to those who were not there to celebrate the new building. Those messages were then tied to helium-filled balloons. As the balloons were released, Rev. Clem said, "We send you our love all the way to heaven."

Dr. Robert Schuller, founder and senior minister of the Crystal Cathedral in Garden Grove, California, has written a book entitled *Life's Not Fair But God Is Good* (Bantam, 1993). The book contains stories about people who have been through all kinds of tragedies and how they have turned tragedy into triumph because of their faith in God.

Dr. Schuller tells about a tragedy in his own family. Several years ago Dr. and Mrs. Schuller were on a preaching mission in Korea when they received a telephone call telling them that their thirteen-year-old daughter, Carol, had been in a motorcycle accident. Carol was riding with a friend when he hit an oncoming car. She was thrown seventy-five feet through the air, and her left leg was left hanging on by a tendon. She was rushed to the hospital, where she was given seventeen pints of blood and very nearly lost her life.

Dr. and Mrs. Schuller immediately flew home, praying all the way for their daughter's life. When they arrived, they discovered that Carol was alive but that the doctors had had to amputate her left leg.

You can imagine the heartache the Schullers felt as they realized their beautiful young daughter would have to go through life without her left leg. But they discovered that even out of this tragedy, God brought something good. Carol grew up as a person of deep faith, and her faithful witness to God's love in spite of her loss has inspired many. Beyond that, she became a person interested in helping other persons with disabilities. Today, she is a happily married mother of two children and an inspiration to others who experience tragedy in their lives.

Through every crucifying experience of life, God is working to bring about new life and hope.

Pause for Reflection

The members of the Goshen United Methodist Church know that life is not fair, but they know more than that. They know that out of the tragedies of life, God brings resurrection and new life to all those who surrender their lives into God's hands. They are people who, through their own experience, believe in the final triumph of righteousness.

Where have you seen victory coming out of tragedy?

Do you know people who have new life and hope coming out of heartache or disappointment in their lives?

When have you had crucifying experiences that led to new opportunities for growth?

Trusting God

Some people seem to have the mistaken belief that if we become Christians, we will never experience heartache or suffering in life. Sometimes we develop the false notion that following Jesus means we will be spared from life's tragedies. Jesus, who was the most faithful human being who ever lived, was not spared from suffering and neither are his followers. Following Christ does not mean that we will never suffer; it only means that we will never suffer alone.

Christians are not people who deny the reality of pain and suffering in this world; rather we are people who can look pain and suffering straight in the eye and walk through it with confidence, trusting God to lead us to greater growth and faith.

A young couple who are members of the church I serve lost their four-year-old daughter Kristin to cancer. For two years she had been through countless radiation treatments, but eventually she lost her life to the disease. Kristin always wanted a picture of Jesus in her hospital room, and her parents would often find her talking to the picture as if she were talking with a close friend. One day she told her parents not to worry about her because she was going to be with Jesus and she would be OK.

Their young daughter's great faith helped the parents through their time of sorrow and grief and loss. They knew she was safe in God's arms, but they still felt incredible pain and sorrow.

Less than a year after the loss of Kristin, this young couple became the parents of a new baby girl. On the first Sunday Amanda was in this world, they brought her to church to thank God for this wonderful gift of new life. As they introduced me to Amanda, tears were running down their cheeks. I know they were remembering Kristin and the pain of her loss, and yet they were filled with joy over the birth of Amanda.

This couple had been through crucifixion; they had faced sorrow and grief squarely and walked through it trusting in God all the way. Now they were experiencing resurrection and new life and new hope in this powerful, wonderful gift from God. Life is not fair, but God is good and brings new life and hope out of every disaster that comes to us in life.

Christians believe in life everlasting. The night before his death, Jesus said: "Do not let your hearts be troubled. Believe in God, believe also in me. In my Father's house there are many dwelling places. If it were not so, would I have told you that I go to prepare a place for you? And if I go and prepare a place for you, I will come again and will take you to myself, so that where I am, there you may be also" (John 14:1-3).

Jesus gives us the assurance that God has prepared a dwelling place for us beyond this life. As Christians, we know that we are more than just a physical body. We know that the essence of our life is in our personality, our spirit, the unique image of God within each of us. When our bodies can carry us no longer, they will return to dust; but the essence of our lives, our spirits, will live on in God's eternal home. This is the life everlasting.

My father died of cancer in March, 1992, at the age of seventy-seven. Shortly before his death, I was sitting beside his hospital bed when he suddenly opened his eyes and said to me, "I just saw my dad." I replied, "Your dad died thirty years ago." He said, "Really? I was just with him over in that bright light. And I'm going to join him. But there are two of us going together. Who do you think the other person is?"

I suggested that it might be Dad's brother because his younger brother was in a hospital 1200 miles away, also suffering with cancer. Dad smiled and said: "Sure, Will is going with me. But I'm not going for two days." Then Dad put his head on the pillow and, with a smile on his face, looked up into the corner of the room as if he were gazing into the light of eternity.

Two hours after that conversation, we received a telephone call telling us that Dad's brother had just died. Two days after that conversation, Dad died. Upon reflection, we realized that Dad had to wait two days because my oldest sister had not yet arrived at his bedside due to difficult flight connections from London. My sister came into Dad's room about 9:00 P.M. They hugged each other and shared their love for each other. Then, about twenty minutes later, Dad breathed his last and entered eternity.

Our family had always believed intellectually in life after death. After Dad's pre-death experience and our conversation with him about it, we knew it to be a reality in our hearts.

Pause for Reflection

Hundreds of people have had pre-death or near-death experiences in which they were given a glimpse of eternity from this side of life. Raymond A. Moody's book *Life After Life* (Walker & Company, 1988) tells the stories of people who have been technically dead for brief periods of time and who have then been revived by modern medical science. These people often report that during those moments when they were technically dead, they had experiences of seeing a bright light, meeting a loved one who had died, or having sensations of peace. After studying hundreds of such cases, some researchers say they are convinced of the reality of life after death.

Modern medical science is simply confirming the truth that Jesus taught in the first century—the spiritual essence of our being lives on beyond death. God breathed God's breath of life into us and that breath is our spirit, which is eternal and everlasting.

Have you known anyone who had a near-death or pre-death experience?

What effect do such stories have on your faith?

What do you believe about eternal life?

In what ways does your belief in eternal life give you hope for the future?